How to Make $500 This Weekend

Setting Up Shop as a Street Vendor

Entrepreneur Series

Muhammad Naveed

Mendon Cottage Books

JD-Biz Publishing

Disclaimer

The information is this book is provided for informational purposes only. It is not intended to be used and medical advice or a substitute for proper medical treatment by a qualified health care provider. The information is believed to be accurate as presented based on research by the author.

The contents have not been evaluated by the U.S. Food and Drug Administration or any other Government or Health Organization and the contents in this book are not to be used to treat cure or prevent disease.

The author or publisher is not responsible for the use or safety of any diet, procedure or treatment mentioned in this book. The author or publisher is not responsible for errors or omissions that may exist.

Warning

The Book is for informational purposes only and before taking on any diet, treatment or medical procedure, it is recommended to consult with your primary health care provider.

Our books are available at

1. Amazon.com
2. Barnes and Noble
3. Itunes
4. Kobo
5. Smashwords
6. Google Play Books

Table of Contents

Introduction

Road vending has become a very popular concept in many cities and people are more often willing to frequent them in their quest for different products and services. They offer quality products at good price ranges. The amount of earnings from their operation can also be healthy and today, more and more enlightened people are becoming interested in getting into the road vending business to earn profits for themselves. This eBook offers instructions on to "How to make $500 this weekend by setting up a shop on the road side (road vending)" and we will be covering all of the aspects related to it. Starting from the advantages, location decision, pricing decisions, and advertising, we will end at the importance of the legal bookkeeping requirements of the business. It will include every major decision making process one should go through before setting up a shop.

This eBook will guide you and provide all the help you might need. It will show you the whole picture of road vending with its exceptional advantages as well as easy-going business and legal requirements.

Advantages of Having a Road Vending Shop

Road vending shops possess hidden advantages over many other shops. Although they are mostly seen as a means of income for those who are not willing to invest much, people can easily earn enough profits to cover their expenses and so forth.

- The biggest advantage is the fact that customers are in front of you, passing by, and thus you can call them over to see your products, which doesn't take them more than ten seconds to do.

- Time is precious for many and when one is able to save time for others, there is no better way to motivate a potential customer to buy a product.

- People selling beverages can take advantage of the opportunity to discern the tastes of people and provide them a different ambience than other formal places.

- Since potential customers find themselves within close proximity to the vendor, it becomes easier to attract them with different advertising techniques. This is not possible with other shops as people are only able to view what is being offered for sale if they actually enter the shop and have enough time to browse the products.

- One other advantage includes of the fact that there is less of an initial investment required. For example, a shop rented by a restaurant is every expensive. However, vendors don't have to pay much to acquire a cart shop. The fee is nominal and also the fee for obtaining a legal permit is not all that much.

- The expenses could be covered and later on adjusted in a way that they can lead the small business to initially break even and then eventually turn a profit.

- The price ranges are also quite flexible for a class of people who don't spend too much. For example, working people might not want to go to an expensive restaurant every day and spend their income on food. Vendors, for them, are a great alternative.

- Since the places that vendors selling food and beverages chose to be at are usually near offices and high traffic areas, it becomes even easier for customers to take advantage of the convenience factor when looking for food and beverages and thus they are more likely to patronize these vendors.

Keeping in mind all these advantages, one can imagine how profitable vending can be, even if it is just being done on the weekend. It is all about how dedicated you are to sell and what you are willing to do to make it happen. Opportunities are available, but taking advantage of the advantages is the responsibility of you and you alone.

Selecting a Business for Roadside Vending

There are two types of business that can be chosen as a guide to establish a roadside business. One is a product-based offering and the other is a service-based offering. A product-based business relies on selling a physical object in the market. It can vary from a book to a machine, food to agricultural products, and so much more. Ascertaining the demand of a certain product is essential before jumping onto the implementation of the business plan. A service-based business denotes a skill or knowledge, an intangible product. Examples include teaching, writing, making websites, and even being a real estate agent or insurance policy provider. There are hundreds of services available that one can provide, but it depends on what skills and knowledge a person acquires about that particular service.

A novel idea directs to the innovation and creation of your own through heavy brainstorming sessions and use of intellectuality. It is not an easy task to just come up with an idea that will not only be possible to implement, but will also create customer demand for it. A very essential skill that an entrepreneur needs to have is to be able to persuade a customer that he/she needs the product or service and encourage them to at least try it once. Creation of such an idea saves the business venture from competition and inflexible pricing range. One can set any pricing that he/she thinks matches their breakeven or generates a functional profit. At the same time, the risk of the business being a success is far greater as well, since no market analysis can be prepared for a product or service that has never been in the market before.

Picking the Right Spot to Set Up Your Shop

The location of a shop matters significantly in determining how effectively you will be able to reach your target audience. It does not matter how small of a business you have, because at the end of the day, the mission of any business is to get as many customers towards your service as possible. Large organizations opt for multiple strategies and take ample time to decide their location because of the importance it carries. Each shop has its own target audience and thus different vending shops will have to set their shop in dedicated areas, wherein they might find potential customers.

Choosing the Right Location is a Key

Location will decide all the factors of your small business and the importance of its chosen location should be seriously considered. Its significance has been defined in detail in the following content. The location decides the type of customers you will be inviting to your shop. For example, if you are setting up a flower vending shop for the weekend near a restaurant, in an area considered as middle-class, then obviously those are the customers who will be targeted. Area matters highly because it will also incorporate the pricing strategy. More than that, quality is one aspect high-class consumers are not willing to compromise on, and thus keeping in mind as to what quality you're providing, location is to be chosen accordingly.

- Tourist Destinations
  The places, where tourists visit can be the best place for the sale of souvenirs and other native arts.

- Office Parks
  These spots are very important and can be used for food stalls.

- Sports Venues
  Sports venues are great places for gathering. You can use this place to set-up a stall and earn through concerned products.

- Empty Lots
  You can set-up your vending shop on an empty lot and can get permission from concerned authorities or the owner of the property.

- Conventions and Conferences
  You can set-up your stall at any conference by obtaining permission from the authorities.

- Public Stations
  You can use a bus stop as well as a train or metro station as a venue to make your earnings.

- Shopping Malls
  You can settle your stall at the entrance of a shopping mall. This will allow you to get the attention of all visitors.

- College and University Campuses
  A college or university campus could be a place for a successful bookstall or other things of students' interest.

Opportunities can be varied from Business to Business

Exploring an area meticulously might help greatly in confirming whether it's the perfect location for you. One might be the utmost perfect location for someone else, but maybe not for you. In understanding almost every strategy that people opt for, you have to comprehend carefully who your potential customers are. For a portrait vending shop, for example, a marketplace would not be suitable at all, whereas a site seeing location might prove helpful with all the tourist traffic. Determining where crowds are most likely to gather and stop to buy if they found something interesting, is a good way to start. Another example for vendors selling foods might be near office buildings from where working people often look for vending shops to get their lunches. Furthermore, coffee has proven to be one basic need for mostly all working people and that being available too, near residential areas or office areas, would gain vendors a large numbers of customers.

Some Unfavorable Places for Road Vending

There are places where vending shops will never be successful like highway roads where people pass through at a high-speed thus missing even the slightest chance of having a look at a vending shop. Freeway exits, on the other hand, are a favorable option for many shops as many people gather and are walking on foot, giving them ample time to take a look at the product or service provided by the vending shops. Always be careful to not setup shops at intersections, as they could be very dangerous or even areas such as a hillside. To maximize the number of customers visiting the shop, you have to give them the ability to do so without the hassle of inconvenient accessibility to your shop.

Choosing a Best Place

The best place all in all, is a location that not only affords pedestrians the flexibility to visit the shop, but automobile traffic as well. This way more people are likely to visit your shop, thus turning leads into successful sales.

However, that is not the only imperative point to remember. What kind of product or service you are selling and the quality of it will determine the best place for your shop. Moving from one place to another might result in a loss of a few customers so strategically deciding a location is a much better idea than experimenting.

How Much to Charge

There is never a right price or standard when selling something unique in the area, where your shop reigns. It is always about the fight between the price you're willing to sell and the price at which the customer is willing to pay and can afford. The demand, quality, and attractiveness of the product or service will decide as to who might be the first, the seller or the buyer, to kneel down for the sake of the brand. Vending shops such as flower vendors usually have fewer cushions in place for price range negotiations, as most people are aware of the premium rates for flowers. So is the case with food stalls set up along the road by different vendors. However, if you have some kind of an artistic jewelry or handbag shop, price diversification is possible.

Location Matters

The most inter-related factor of pricing is the location of the shop. Location counters different class groups, might pertain to either just one socio economic class, or probably a mix of two or three considering that your shop is at a place where different kinds of customers pass by. Freeway exits are one of those places possibly. Since location is a big factor in determining the price range, you'll be able to uphold for your products, and incorporate both the decisions together when planning the setup of a road vending shop.

Don't Forget to Include Overheads in Pricing Strategies

Firstly, the amount you'll be charging your customers for each product should accustom a part of the costs incurred in setting up the shop, buying the inventory, and all other landing costs. That would mean incorporating both direct and indirect costs as much as possible. That obviously doesn't mean that your customers will understand what you have done and cooperate by paying what you want them to pay. Rather you have to opt for a mix of pricing strategies such as keeping them low at the start to bring in the traffic or choosing a rate which allows you to breakeven for a few months and then when all initial fixed costs are covered, consequently the remaining would be the profit attained. The initial fixed costs could probably be the application fee for the vending shop and the shop accessories itself. Variable costs, for example, for a beverage vending shop would be the daily costs of buying the beverages from the wholesale market. On the other hand, the costs of setting up a portrait sketching shop might only be of fixed costs as the products one would purchase there are mostly a once in a year type of purchase. It always varies on the type of vending shop you have and the decision is to be made accordingly.

Think about Your Competitors

Competition is one other factor to consider when setting prices for your goods; that is if you have any. If the location you think is the best for you already has a similar vending shop in close proximity, then there are other considerations you have to look for. These other factors are the prices, the quality they offer, and other discounts they give in order to provide incentive for the customers to buy and each of their other visible strategies. When all's said and done, the value of the profits will determine as to how effectively you managed to triumph over your competition, and as a result the prospects.

Do You Need a License?

Running a vending shop is similar to handling a business. The difference is that with a vending shop, all the affairs are transacted in front of the customers and it usually comes in the form of a very small business venture that is operated in order to earn extra money. A vending shop just cannot be set-up anywhere, anytime, or any type of way, but rather a professional procedure is to be followed to acquire such accessibility on the roads. There are stringent rules and regulations for vending shops, which have to be followed by every vendor. Different cities have their own set of regulations, which should be followed by the citizens and known through the directory or the internet.

A Permit May be Required

A legal permit has to be acquired to set up a shop at a particular location, whether you're occupying a minimal space or bigger. A legal permit for most cities usually means a road-vending certificate. In other words, you could term that as having a license for vending shops. The license, as many others, is usually good for a year and has to be renewed beforehand if one is planning to keep the shop at the same location. It is always a better option to not leave this part for the last minute, because the regulatory authorities sell available locations mostly on a first come/first serve basis. If you have chosen a place, go ahead and sign for it instantly before anyone else grabs it.

Don't Sign the Permit before Obtaining a Suitable Venue

Before choosing the location and thus signing the permit, you have to be very careful to adhere to the regulations set by the authorities, as not every place allows for the operation of such vending shops. There are certain areas and intersections where vendors can put up their shops and that too with additional rules such as the area size. It would be inappropriate to set up in residential areas. Usually, enough space is allotted to vendors to set-up their shops in the way they might please, say as much as the space of one parking spot. To ensure peace and ease to all citizens, these laws have been dignified.

Read the Rules and Regulations Carefully

To avoid any litigation you must read your city's rules of road vending scrupulously, especially if and whether you're allowed to have electrical devices or packaged foods etc. In addition, stopping potential customers in the middle of the road is prohibited for safety concerns and thus a customer has to stop at the parking stops only to get your product. This is also the one reason why choosing a location that caters to automobile traffic with elasticity is highly imperative.

Apart from these regulations, there are hardly any rules which one authority can impose on your pricing or other strategies of the shop, like how to run the small business you have taken the initiative to set up. Those considerations are completely up to you. However, roads weren't primarily made for this purpose and thus the authority has to be very careful of the decision to grant permission to operate a vending shop. Therefore, your dedication to the shop should be authentic enough for the authorities to see that you'll abide by the laws set and be of a good nature to all citizens. The clauses clearly mention such statements in the permit you'll be required to obtain.

How to Advertise

The norm of traditional advertising includes newspaper, flyers, television, radio, etc. However, internet technologies have taken over a huge market on the basis of less cost vs. more benefit. In this case though, where we are talking chiefly about road vending, any of these methods would unlikely result in the effective generation of traffic towards their shop. This is because such shops are not likely to be searched by potential customers; if they appear in front of them they'll visit it, otherwise they won't be spending much of their time searching. Even if one still wants to post an advertisement, it might not be economical as they are extremely expensive advertisement methods. For example, in the case of a hot dog vendor shop, in the morning people will probably just look for it on their way to work or school, but no one would especially type into a search engine to find out its location. Hand-made jewelry designs and antique items, if seen by a number of tourists, are likely to be bought by them at that point in time only.

Get the Attention of People by any Means

Therefore, the ultimate aim should be attracting and diverting the attention of those passing by with instant methods. Some might just come to you on their own will, but for most of them, you have to invite them by advertising and letting them know of your existence. This is the true in-depth nature of advertising tested on people because they have to be very spontaneous and on the edge for the entire time that they're selling their product. The conclusion is that drawing attention through diversified methods will get you more customers than sitting around, waiting for customers to arrive at your location.

Use the Right Material to Attract Buyers

Signs are a form of advertising generally utilized by almost all vendors for the passer-by to read and be familiar with the main product you're selling. Signs can be made in a superior way in lieu of being written with pens, markers, or unprofessional paint, as it might give an impression of low quality on the basis of low enthusiasm. Thus, hand-written signs look funky and are likely to attract more customers. Moreover, you can easily be creative by creating signs that draw attention and laughter both at the same time. Be very careful with the font sizes, as people from a relative distance should be able to view it and come towards your shop. Also, the professionally printed or painted signs will not give the look of a small business, possibly family-oriented, and this perception might shoo away the middle-class customers looking for reasonable prices.

Discounts and Sales Attract Buyers

For a few vendor shops, such as hot dog vendors, customers will probably become loyal and in order to make sure that they are satisfied, it's better to offer discounted rates and other offers if possible. Staying in contact with them through social media can also be very helpful. Local newspapers are also a possibility if you're new around the shop. You might want to at least let them know about your vendor shop and then it is up to them to post it or not. Whichever the case, it is always worth a try.

Some Unique Ideas for Advertisement

Other than that, a few out-of-the-box advertising methods could be used such as wearing costumes that represent your shop better than the shop itself. This has been opted by many, and has been proven successful in easily attracting customers. Colorful funny costumes or any traditional wear can allure the customers with its originality. Dancing around or singing a related song could also divert attention of many people, thus making them potential customers. A little push of creativity can change the whole scenario for you. However, it might not work everywhere, but the point of trying is not to attract all customers, but some who might have otherwise passed by without even looking.

Payment Methods

When it comes to payment for products, a dilemma takes its route sometimes with no effect, whereas sometimes it can lead to the loss of a few potential customers. The general payment options for buying a product at any usual store would be cash, credit card, debit card, online payment through PayPal, or any other related service. All these options make it easier for customers to buy the product with ease and flexibility. Credit cards are very popular in most countries for shopping and tourists often prefer using their cards over cash since they carry them with them all the time and they are widely recognized.

Try to Get Paid on the Spot, as it is Most Likely that the Buyer will Never Come Back

If one is setting up a road vending shop, the possibility of affording the credit card facility to the customers becomes very difficult. In addition, the products vending shops offer are usually much lower-priced, making cash the preferred method of payment by vendors. This, however, might discourage some customers who might not be carrying enough cash at the moment, but that is quite unlikely as well because like already mentioned prices are quite low. Moreover, the things road vendors sell are not the things that people would go back to get the cash and come to buy. Therefore, once you lose the customer, you have lost them for good. This is not mostly an issue for road vendors who provide foods and beverages because people tend to pay by cash when they come to buy these sorts of beverages on the way from the office or school or any other place. Many working people purchase lunches from these vending shops. It is for other items such as "vintage collectibles" that this might be an issue because a good number of customers are likely to be tourists and they mostly only carry their credit cards with them.

PayPal Can be a Perfect Alternative

Apart from all these, there is one incredible option available for the vendors if they can somehow can get access to an internet connection through Wi-Fi or otherwise. PayPal is internet-based software, which allows you to transfer money from the customers to the sellers. For such transactions, one needs to have a PayPal account, which can be made without any trouble. Today, it is being used by large organization as well, to get the important transactions done. Most of the online businesses run on the basis of it as well, and Road vendors can use their laptops and the internet connection to do so, thus availing all the customers coming to them. Most of the road vendors have been doing this, so there is no doubt that it helps.

For better provision and customer enhancement, you can keep your options open to cash and online payments. Since, road vending is not an easy job and customers are hard to get sometimes, it would be in a vendor's best interest to give customers the highest flexibility in all terms and that includes the mode of payment as well.

How to Set-Up Shop at the County Fair or Swap Meet

County fairs are the best place to set up vending shops because of un-quantified advantages over shops at usual places. They not only provide the ambience for people to shop, eat, and have fun, but also elevate the opportunity of vendors to utilize their time more productively in aim of earning a good, healthy amount. The point is, people come to these fairs to spend money so if you can them attract them successfully with your product, and lure them in with enhanced creative methods then you're in for the best possible earnings from operating at a county fair or swap meet.

Weekend County Fairs and Swap Meets

There are usually many county fairs and swap meets going on within a city at one time, especially during the weekends. The weekend presents a good opportunity for sales because that is the time families enjoy an outing to these events and also people are free from their work, thus they are invigorated and excited to find something worth their money. You can look into newspapers and magazines to keep updated about any events happening around the city and an internet search would also provide ample information on the list of events with duration.

Choose a Fair that Attracts More People and Suits your Product

A scrupulous look in every county fair is important before deciding where to set the shop. Different areas attract different kinds of customers of different socio-economic backgrounds. In addition, people with different tastes are always present at county fairs or swap meets. You should examine, which county fair or swap meet attracts the highest number of people and also what kind of people might be your potential customers. However, it is obviously not imposed on you to only sign at only one county fair, so you can also experiment in different areas of events, meticulously observing where you benefited the most.

Be Aware of the Rules

Setting up a shop requires the fulfillment of certain forms, and the ability to abide by the rules and regulations of the authority of that particular county fair or swap meet. These usually include the permit or certificate of vending shops. Other requirements depend on which county fair you're going to be vending. The stalls are assigned on a first come/first serve basis and can be attained through walk-in interviews at the administration department. They are quite stringent on the paper filling procedure, so ensure you have everything they require of you by checking their necessities written in the form. The time duration, day, and space will be mentioned in the document given to you by them, which will give you the authorization to set up your shop.

Some Fees You May Incur

The events charge a fee for the application and it varies from one place to another. The fee is not usually very high and for vendors they are even less expensive. Vendors can accommodate the fee and increase the prices a bit, consequently resulting in a profit. Alternatively, if you get many customers and make successful sales then you would not have to increase the price, in case the customers are driven away by the prices. It is all about acting instantly accordingly to the environment and the willingness of customers.

Get Ready for a Competition

There are many stalls at all county fairs meaning the competition is as high as it could be. Therefore, differentiation is important; in either the product you're selling or the way that you're selling it. People selling paintings, antique items, and jewelry usually dress nicely and attractively, inviting people elegantly to come and see the stock. Others can wear costumes and use other advertising techniques to catch the attention of as many customers as possible. It is always better to offer diversified products so as to suit the taste of different potential customers. Also, make sure the price range of most of your products suits the type of people coming to that county fair as people come to these places with the expectation that they'll find desired products for less than they would at other stores.

Importance of Bookkeeping

When someone hears the word "bookkeeping", fear instills into his or her mind instantly without even considering the ulterior possibility. In real terms, it is not even difficult to keep the track record of your own business yourself. It consists of only knowing about a few concepts to help you draw the book, maintain it according to legal terms, and keep doing it for as long as the business survives. There have been facts drawn upon the fact that every other successful business always has a legal book through which they make strategic plans on how to sustain the business venture.

Bookkeeping is Simple

The bookkeeping process simply includes inputting the figures concerning all income and expenses in a systematic way so as to generate results about how effective resources have been used, in order to earn profits, or end in loss otherwise. These financial records of the business help in identifying many issues a business might have and the drawbacks. This is important because if you don't know what the drawbacks are, how are you supposed to work on them to find the alternative solutions? Also, maintaining cash flow in proper order helps in making business decisions pertaining to the road-vending weekend.

Keep a Record of Your Earnings

In literal terms, bookkeeping involves the use of accounts and basic accounting terms to help keep records of the financial affairs of the business. A cashbook should be created in which you'll note down all the inflows and outflows of the business. A sales ledger to track down all the money you have received and any amount of cash you might owe to someone should also be kept. A purchase ledger is recommended for recording all the outflows of the business and lastly a wages book for payments like salary, etc.

When talking in terms of road vending, although the accounts will most probably be not that complex, maintaining them still might take time for people who have been newly introduced to such work. Yet, with dedication, in no time anybody can get the hang of it. The outflows of the vending shop will probably include the inventory, carts, other supplies, etc. It all depends on what kind of road vending shop you'll be operating for the weekend in order to earn $500. If you have a hot dog vending shop then the inventory will consists of a difficult stock to handle, because obviously each day of the weekend, fresh stock will be coming in and maybe not all being used. How would you know exactly how many sausages you should order each day? The answer involves viewing the number of sales made in what price ranges and comparing it to the prices at which you're getting the sausages; all of these will help you determine the selling price of your product and how much inventory you're supposed to keep for each day.

Record Keeping is Important

That was just one example of how important bookkeeping is for a business. When people come into practical circumstances, they understand the superior advantages bookkeeping contributes to the success of the business. The outflows usually are many and with road vending, keeping track of all of them in your mind is not a job that can be done without making errors at the end of the day. There are additional calculations that can be done with the help of the book to figure out how much you're supposed to sell in order to achieve a breakeven in the short-term business and consequently profits.

You can Figure out the Best Place for Vending

With road vending, often experiments are done by selling at different places each day or weekend. How would you know, in exact facts and figures, as to where your business performed better considering all the costs that incurred at each place? Bookkeeping in this sense helps significantly. Each place has its own operating costs, for example, the amount it costs to rent the location. Accustoming all the fixed costs and then comparing them to the sales made is not just a simple math calculation of two plus two four and this is why bookkeeping has been given such importance in the world of business.

Professional Accountancy is not Essential

Legal bookkeeping refers to following the standard rules set by authorities so that the records of each business are kept in the same way so as to being able to compare the performance of the business throughout the year. Road vending, possibly, might not need to be compared with other businesses, but since rules have been established and you're making the effort to maintain a business cashbook, regulations should be thus followed. At any time, for example, at a county fair or swap meet, you will want the authorities to see that you have maintained a capable business until now; bookkeeping would be the best proof of that.

Conclusion

The mission of this eBook was to inform you and help you acknowledge the aspects of road vending. All chapters have been covered duly and in detail so as to leave you with no difficult questions unanswered. The major decisions and possibilities have been discussed, each meticulously, to guide you in making as much profit as possible within the road vending business.

If one follows this eBook one-step at a time and without missing the small details, which might seem small, but are highly significant to the business, earning $500 within a weekend of road vending would be a realistic goal. People can easily take advantage of this amazing opportunity to earn to cover their expenses or enjoy a vacation. Road vending also could be taken as a fun activity as it requires interaction with people in a manner, which is not only alluring, but also enjoyable to the vendor himself. Whichever reason one chooses to opt for a vending business, it is always about dedication to the business, which guides a person to the highest level of success.

Author Bio

Muhammad Naveed is proficient writer and engaged in article and book writing for last 5 years. During this time, he has produced over 10,000 blogs Journal articles and eBooks on various niches related to travel, make money, real estate, biography and well-being. He is a regular contributor to several blogs and article directories. He is the editor of several blogs and newspapers.

Check out some of the other JD-Biz Publishing books

Gardening Series on Amazon

Health Learning Series

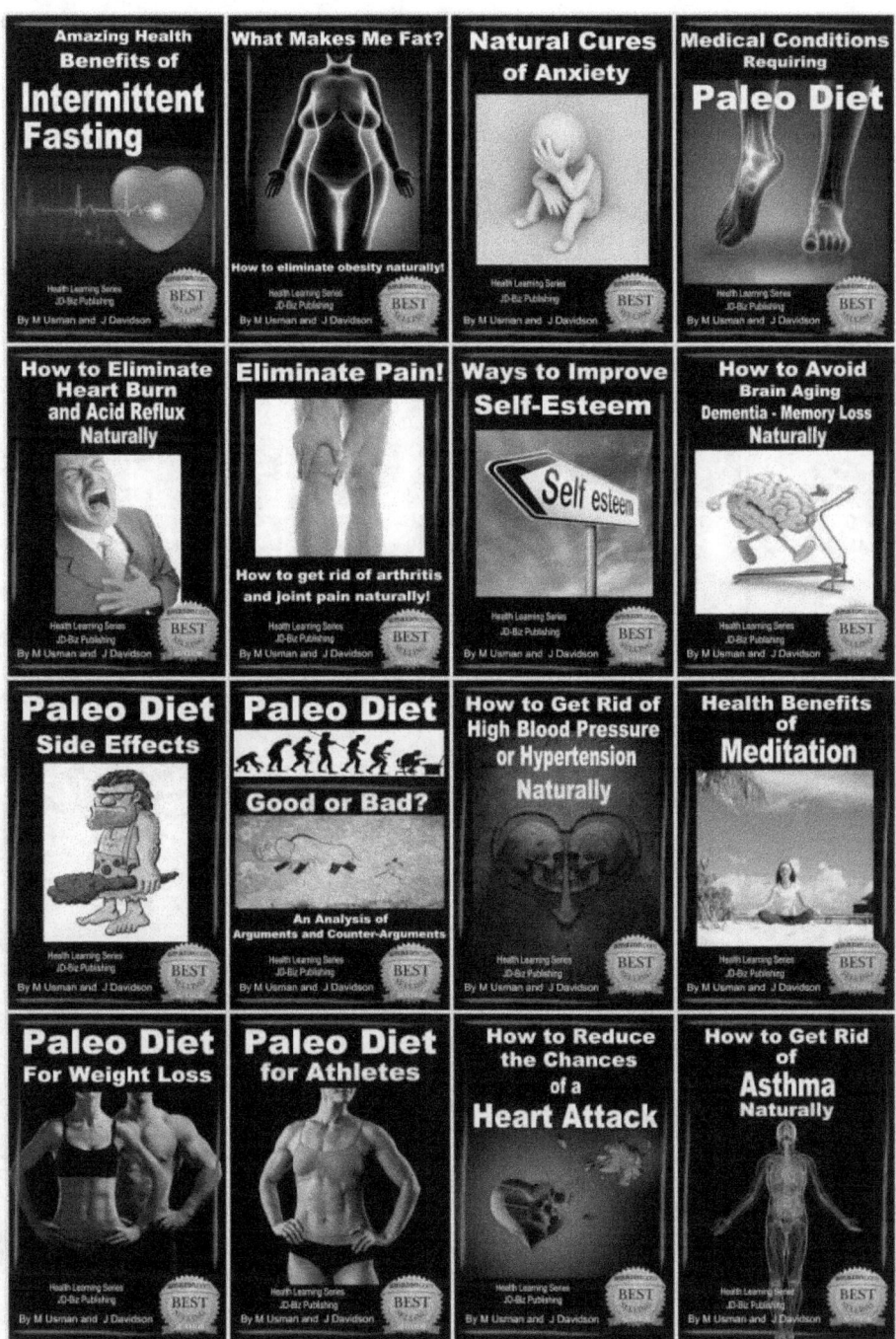

Amazing Animal Book Series

How to Build and Plan Books

Entrepreneur Book Series

Our books are available at

1. Amazon.com

2. Barnes and Noble

3. Itunes

4. Kobo

5. Smashwords

6. Google Play Books

Publisher

JD-Biz Corp

P O Box 374

Mendon, Utah 84325

http://www.jd-biz.com/

Mendon Cottage Books

P O Box 374, Mendon Utah 84325

www.ingramcontent.com/pod-product-compliance
Lightning Source LLC
Chambersburg PA
CBHW071017180526
45168CB00003B/1463